Native American Life

# Longhouses

by Karen Bush Gibson

**Consultant:**
Mike Wahrare Tarbell
Educator, Iroquois Indian Museum
Howe's Cave, New York

Capstone
press

Mankato, Minnesota

Bridgestone Books are published by Capstone Press,
151 Good Counsel Drive, P.O. Box 669, Mankato, Minnesota 56002.
www.capstonepress.com

*Library of Congress Cataloging-in-Publication Data*
Gibson, Karen Bush.
Longhouses / by Karen Bush Gibson.
    p. cm.—(Bridgestone books. Native American life)
    Includes bibliographical references and index.
    ISBN 0-7368-3724-8 (hardcover)
    1. Indians of North America—Dwellings. 2. Longhouses—North America. I. Title. II. Series:
Bridgestone Books: Native American life (Mankato, Minn.)
E98.D9G52 2005
728'.312—dc22                                                          2004011214

Summary: A brief introduction to longhouses, including the materials, construction, and people who
    lived in these traditional Native American dwellings.

**Editorial Credits**
Roberta Basel and Katy Kudela, editors; Jennifer Bergstrom, designer; Wanda Winch, photo researcher;
    Scott Thoms, photo editor

**Photo Credits**
Bridgeman Art Library/French Explorer's Council with Indians (At the Iroquois Council Fire) c. 1901,
Remington, Frederic (1861–1909), Museum of Fine Arts, Houston, Texas/Hogg Brothers Collection,
Gift of Miss Ima Hogg, 18; Canadian Museum of Civilization/by Roberta Wilson, photo Harry Foster,
image no. D2004–18606, 14; Corbis/Nathan Benn, 20; James P. Rowan, cover, 1, 4, 12; Photo courtesy
of Carol Sheehan, 8; Stock Montage Inc., 6; With the Permission of the Royal Ontario Museum©ROM,
10, 16

1  2  3  4  5  6  10  09  08  07  06  05

# Table of Contents

# What Is a Longhouse?

Longhouses are narrow wooden houses built by Native Americans. These houses were built with straight sides and curved roofs. Longhouses had doorways at each end but no windows.

The number of people living in a longhouse decided its length. Most houses were 20 feet (6 meters) wide and 20 feet (6 meters) tall. But they could be longer than a football field.

◄ Longhouses were houses built with wood and bark from cedar and elm trees.

# Who Lived in a Longhouse?

Longhouses were the homes of Native Americans who lived in what is now the northeastern United States and southern Canada. The Iroquois were the largest group of longhouse builders.

As many as 20 families could live in a single longhouse. These families were part of a **clan**. They were all related through a woman called the clan mother.

Today, the Iroquois no longer live in these houses. But the longhouse is still important. People use longhouses for special gatherings.

◄ The Iroquois called themselves "Haudenosaunee." This name means "people of the longhouse."

# Gathering Materials

The Iroquois went into the forest to find materials for their longhouse. Men chopped down cedar and elm trees. Builders used this wood for the **frame** of the house.

The Iroquois also peeled large sheets of bark from trees. Women gathered bark in late spring when it was easier to peel. They used the bark to cover the sides and roof of the longhouse.

◄ Tree bark was a building material. Iroquois women peeled bark from trees in the forest.

# Preparing the Materials

The Iroquois dried out the sheets of bark. They placed heavy stones on top of the sheets. The stones kept the bark flat until it was dry and ready to use.

The Iroquois prepared other materials. Some people cut strips of bark to make lacing. They used lacing to tie sheets of bark to the frame. Other people cut pieces of wood into posts. People also made glue from deerskins. Builders used glue to hold the wood poles together.

◀ Men carefully cut wood poles for the longhouse.

# Building a Longhouse

The first step in building a longhouse was to choose a flat space. Builders cleared the land of trees and brush. They then set thick wood posts in the ground. These posts formed the outside walls and center **aisle**. They then tied poles to the outside walls and bent them to make a dome roof.

Finally, the builders covered the roof and sides of the longhouse with bark. They made small holes in the roof called smoke holes.

◄ Builders used wood posts and poles to make the frame of a longhouse.

14

# Inside a Longhouse

Each family had its own area in the longhouse. They built platforms along the walls. People used these raised areas to work, sleep, and store food and supplies.

The Iroquois built fires in the center of the longhouse. Two families shared each fire. They used the fires for cooking, heating, and light. Smoke from the fires escaped through the smoke holes in the roof.

◀ Many families lived together in a longhouse.

# Longhouse Villages

The Iroquois built different sized villages. Some villages had only a few longhouses. Other villages had 200 longhouses.

The Iroquois built walls around their villages. They built 20-foot (6-meter) walls with pointed wood posts. These **palisades** protected the village from enemies and wild animals.

The Iroquois moved about every 20 years. They moved to another area and built new longhouses. They believed moving to a new place gave the earth time to rest.

◄ A wall of wooden posts helped to protect a village.

## Special Longhouses

Each village had a special longhouse owned by the chief. It was usually the largest longhouse in the village. The chief's home was a place to welcome visitors from other **nations**. Leaders met in the chief's house to talk. People in the village also came to this longhouse for **ceremonies**.

People built some longhouses as a place to prepare food. They sometimes used these longhouses to store food.

◄ A chief's longhouse was a place for leaders and visitors to meet and talk.

# Iroquois Confederacy

The longhouse was the **symbol** of the Iroquois **Confederacy**. Nations making up this group were the Mohawk, Oneida, Seneca, Onondaga, and Cayuga. Nations in the confederacy believed they were like families in one large longhouse.

The longhouse was an important part of the Iroquois Confederacy more than 500 years ago. Many people made these long narrow buildings their homes. Today, some nations still build modern longhouses for meetings and ceremonies.

◄ The Iroquois still use longhouses for ceremonies.

# Glossary

aisle (ILE)—a walkway between seats or living areas in a longhouse

ceremony (SER-uh-moh-nee)—formal actions, words, and often music performed to mark an important occasion

clan (KLAN)—a large group of related families

confederacy (kuhn-FED-ur-uh-see)—a union of people or tribes with a common goal

frame (FRAYM)—the basic shape over which a house is built

nation (NAY-shun)—a tribe, or a group of people, who live in the same area and speak the same language

palisade (pal-uh-SAYD)—a tall fence that protects an Iroquois village from wind, animals, and enemy attacks

symbol (SIM-buhl)—an object that stands for something else

# Read More

**Beres, Cynthia Breslin.** *Longhouse.* Native American Homes. Vero Beach, Fla.: Rourke, 2001.

**Koestler-Grack, Rachel A.** *The Iroquois: Longhouse Builders.* America's First Peoples. Mankato, Minn.: Blue Earth Books, 2003.

# Internet Sites

FactHound offers a safe, fun way to find Internet sites related to this book. All of the sites on FactHound have been researched by our staff.

Here's how:
1. Visit *www.facthound.com*
2. Type in this special code **0736837248** for age-appropriate sites. Or enter a search word related to this book for a more general search.
3. Click on the **Fetch It** button.

FactHound will fetch the best sites for you!

# Index